_____
_____
_____
_____
_____
_____
_____
_____
_____
_____
_____
_____
_____
_____
_____
_____
_____
_____
_____
_____
_____
_____
_____
_____
_____

He makes me lie down in green pastures;
He leads me beside the still waters.
Psalm 23:2

Before the mountains were brought forth, or ever You had formed
the earth and the world, even from everlasting to everlasting, You are God.
Psalm 90:2

He is our God, and we are the people of His pasture,
and the sheep of His hand.
Psalm 95:7

C

The LORD is my rock and my fortress and my deliverer;
my God, my strength, in whom I will trust.
Psalm 18:2

He makes my feet like the feet of deer,
and sets me on my high places.
Psalm 18:33

Mercy and truth have met together;
righteousness and peace have kissed each other.
Psalm 85:10

_____

_____

_____

_____

_____

_____

_____

_____

_____

_____

_____

_____

_____

_____

_____

_____

_____

_____

_____

_____

_____

_____

_____

_____

LORD, You have been our
dwelling place in all generations.
Psalm 90:1

I will instruct you and teach you in the way you should go;
I will guide you with My eye.
Psalm 32:8

He loves righteousness and justice;
the earth is full of the goodness of the LORD.
Psalm 33:5

Trust in the LORD, and do good;
dwell in the land, and feed on His faithfulness.
Psalm 37:3

Delight yourself also in the LORD,
and He shall give you the desires of your heart.
Psalm 37:4

My soul longs, yes, even faints for the courts of the LORD;
my heart and my flesh cry out for the living God.
Psalm 84:2

For a day in Your courts
is better than a thousand.
Psalm 84:10

Trust in Him at all times, you people;
pour out your heart before Him; God is a refuge for us. Selah
Psalm 62:8

Whom have I in heaven but You?
And there is none upon earth that I desire besides You.
Psalm 73:25

Oh, taste and see that the LORD is good;
blessed is the man who trusts in Him!
Psalm 34:8

Your mercy, O LORD, is in the heavens,
your faithfulness reaches to the clouds.
Psalm 36:5

But He made His own people go forth like sheep, and guided them in the wilderness like a flock;
And He led them on safely, so that they did not fear; but the sea overwhelmed their enemies.
Psalm 78:52-53

So we, Your people and sheep of Your pasture,
will give You thanks forever.
Psalm 79:13

How precious is Your lovingkindness, O God! Therefore the children
of men put their trust under the shadow of Your wings:
Psalm 36:7

For with You is the fountain of life;
in Your light we see light.
Psalm 36:9

C

My voice You shall hear in the morning, O LORD;
in the morning I will direct it to You, and I will look up.
Psalm 5:3

In Your presence is fullness of joy;
at Your right hand are pleasures forevermore.
Psalm 16:11

LORD, I have loved the habitation of Your house,
and the place where Your glory dwells.
Psalm 26:8

The LORD will give strength to His people;
the LORD will bless His people with peace.
Psalm 29:11

The LORD will command His lovingkindness in the daytime and in the
night His song shall be with me—a prayer to the God of my life.
Psalm 42:8

My soul, wait silently for God alone,
for my expectation is from Him.
Psalm 62:5

Exalt the LORD our God, and worship at His holy hill;
for the LORD our God is holy.
Psalm 99:9

We are His people
and the sheep of His pasture.
Psalm 100:3

Rest in the LORD,
and wait patiently for Him.
Psalm 37:7

As the deer pants for the water brooks,
so pants my soul for You, O God.
Psalm 42:1

The LORD is my shepherd;
I shall not want.
Psalm 23:1

He makes me lie down in green pastures;
He leads me beside the still waters.
Psalm 23:2

Before the mountains were brought forth, or ever You had formed
the earth and the world, even from everlasting to everlasting, You are God.
Psalm 90:2

He is our God, and we are the people of His pasture,
and the sheep of His hand.
Psalm 95:7

The LORD is my rock and my fortress and my deliverer;
my God, my strength, in whom I will trust.
Psalm 18:2

He makes my feet like the feet of deer,
and sets me on my high places.
Psalm 18:33

Mercy and truth have met together;
righteousness and peace have kissed each other.
Psalm 85:10

LORD, You have been our
dwelling place in all generations.
Psalm 90:1

I will instruct you and teach you in the way you should go;
I will guide you with My eye.
Psalm 32:8

_____

_____

_____

_____

_____

_____

_____

_____

_____

_____

_____

_____

_____

_____

_____

_____

_____

_____

_____

_____

_____

_____

_____

_____

He loves righteousness and justice;
the earth is full of the goodness of the LORD.
Psalm 33:5

Trust in the LORD, and do good;
dwell in the land, and feed on His faithfulness.
Psalm 37:3

Delight yourself also in the LORD,
and He shall give you the desires of your heart.
Psalm 37:4

C

My soul longs, yes, even faints for the courts of the LORD;
my heart and my flesh cry out for the living God.
Psalm 84:2

For a day in Your courts
is better than a thousand.
Psalm 84:10

Trust in Him at all times, you people;
pour out your heart before Him; God is a refuge for us. Selah
Psalm 62:8

Whom have I in heaven but You?
And there is none upon earth that I desire besides You.
Psalm 73:25

C

Oh, taste and see that the LORD is good;
blessed is the man who trusts in Him!
Psalm 34:8

_____

_____

_____

_____

_____

_____

_____

_____

_____

_____

_____

_____

_____

_____

_____

_____

_____

_____

_____

_____

_____

_____

Your mercy, O LORD, is in the heavens,
your faithfulness reaches to the clouds.
Psalm 36:5

But He made His own people go forth like sheep, and guided them in the wilderness like a flock;
And He led them on safely, so that they did not fear; but the sea overwhelmed their enemies.
Psalm 78:52-53

So we, Your people and sheep of Your pasture,
will give You thanks forever.
Psalm 79:13

How precious is Your lovingkindness, O God! Therefore the children
of men put their trust under the shadow of Your wings:
Psalm 36:7

For with You is the fountain of life;
in Your light we see light.
Psalm 36:9

C

My voice You shall hear in the morning, O LORD;
in the morning I will direct it to You, and I will look up.
Psalm 5:3

In Your presence is fullness of joy;
at Your right hand are pleasures forevermore.
Psalm 16:11

LORD, I have loved the habitation of Your house,
and the place where Your glory dwells.
Psalm 26:8

The LORD will give strength to His people;
the LORD will bless His people with peace.
Psalm 29:11

The LORD will command His lovingkindness in the daytime and in the
night His song shall be with me—a prayer to the God of my life.
Psalm 42:8

My soul, wait silently for God alone,
for my expectation is from Him.
Psalm 62:5

Exalt the LORD our God, and worship at His holy hill;
for the LORD our God is holy.
Psalm 99:9

We are His people
and the sheep of His pasture.
Psalm 100:3

Rest in the LORD,
and wait patiently for Him.
Psalm 37:7

As the deer pants for the water brooks,
so pants my soul for You, O God.
Psalm 42:1

The LORD is my shepherd;
I shall not want.
Psalm 23:1

_____

_____

_____

_____

_____

_____

_____

_____

_____

_____

_____

_____

_____

_____

_____

_____

_____

_____

_____

_____

_____

_____

_____

_____

He makes me lie down in green pastures;
He leads me beside the still waters.
Psalm 23:2

Before the mountains were brought forth, or ever You had formed
the earth and the world, even from everlasting to everlasting, You are God.
Psalm 90:2

He is our God, and we are the people of His pasture,
and the sheep of His hand.
Psalm 95:7

The LORD is my rock and my fortress and my deliverer;
my God, my strength, in whom I will trust.
Psalm 18:2

He makes my feet like the feet of deer,
and sets me on my high places.
Psalm 18:33

Mercy and truth have met together;
righteousness and peace have kissed each other.
Psalm 85:10

LORD, You have been our
dwelling place in all generations.
Psalm 90:1

I will instruct you and teach you in the way you should go;
I will guide you with My eye.
Psalm 32:8

_____

_____

_____

_____

_____

_____

_____

_____

_____

_____

_____

_____

_____

_____

_____

_____

_____

_____

_____

_____

_____

_____

He loves righteousness and justice;
the earth is full of the goodness of the LORD.
Psalm 33:5

Trust in the LORD, and do good;
dwell in the land, and feed on His faithfulness.
Psalm 37:3

Delight yourself also in the LORD,
and He shall give you the desires of your heart.
Psalm 37:4

My soul longs, yes, even faints for the courts of the LORD;
my heart and my flesh cry out for the living God.
Psalm 84:2

For a day in Your courts
is better than a thousand.
Psalm 84:10

Trust in Him at all times, you people;
pour out your heart before Him; God is a refuge for us. Selah
Psalm 62:8

Whom have I in heaven but You?
And there is none upon earth that I desire besides You.
Psalm 73:25

Oh, taste and see that the LORD is good;
blessed is the man who trusts in Him!
Psalm 34:8

Your mercy, O LORD, is in the heavens,
your faithfulness reaches to the clouds.
Psalm 36:5

But He made His own people go forth like sheep, and guided them in the wilderness like a flock;
And He led them on safely, so that they did not fear; but the sea overwhelmed their enemies.
Psalm 78:52-53

So we, Your people and sheep of Your pasture,
will give You thanks forever.
Psalm 79:13

How precious is Your lovingkindness, O God! Therefore the children
of men put their trust under the shadow of Your wings.
Psalm 36:7

For with You is the fountain of life;
in Your light we see light.
Psalm 36:9

My voice You shall hear in the morning, O LORD;
in the morning I will direct it to You, and I will look up.
Psalm 5:3

In Your presence is fullness of joy;
at Your right hand are pleasures forevermore.
Psalm 16:11

LORD, I have loved the habitation of Your house,
and the place where Your glory dwells.
Psalm 26:8

The LORD will give strength to His people;
the LORD will bless His people with peace.
Psalm 29:11

The LORD will command His lovingkindness in the daytime and in the
night His song shall be with me—a prayer to the God of my life.
Psalm 42:8

My soul, wait silently for God alone,
for my expectation is from Him.
Psalm 62:5

Exalt the LORD our God, and worship at His holy hill;
for the LORD our God is holy.
Psalm 99:9

We are His people
and the sheep of His pasture.
Psalm 100:3

Rest in the LORD,
and wait patiently for Him.
Psalm 37:7

As the deer pants for the water brooks,
so pants my soul for You, O God.
Psalm 42:1

The LORD is my shepherd;
I shall not want.
Psalm 23:1

He makes me lie down in green pastures;
He leads me beside the still waters.
Psalm 23:2

Before the mountains were brought forth, or ever You had formed
the earth and the world, even from everlasting to everlasting, You are God.
Psalm 90:2

He is our God, and we are the people of His pasture,
and the sheep of His hand.
Psalm 95:7

The LORD is my rock and my fortress and my deliverer;
my God, my strength, in whom I will trust.
Psalm 18:2

He makes my feet like the feet of deer,
and sets me on my high places.
Psalm 18:33

Mercy and truth have met together;
righteousness and peace have kissed each other.
Psalm 85:10

LORD, You have been our
dwelling place in all generations.
Psalm 90:1

I will instruct you and teach you in the way you should go;
I will guide you with My eye.
Psalm 32:8

He loves righteousness and justice;
the earth is full of the goodness of the LORD.
Psalm 33:5

Trust in the LORD, and do good;
dwell in the land, and feed on His faithfulness.
Psalm 37:3

Delight yourself also in the LORD,
and He shall give you the desires of your heart.
Psalm 37:4

My soul longs, yes, even faints for the courts of the LORD;
my heart and my flesh cry out for the living God.
Psalm 84:2

For a day in Your courts
is better than a thousand.
Psalm 84:10

Trust in Him at all times, you people;
pour out your heart before Him; God is a refuge for us. Selah
Psalm 62:8

Whom have I in heaven but You?
And there is none upon earth that I desire besides You.
Psalm 73:25

Oh, taste and see that the LORD is good;
blessed is the man who trusts in Him!
Psalm 34:8

Your mercy, O LORD, is in the heavens,
your faithfulness reaches to the clouds.
Psalm 36:5

But He made His own people go forth like sheep, and guided them in the wilderness like a flock;
And He led them on safely, so that they did not fear; but the sea overwhelmed their enemies.
Psalm 78:52-53

So we, Your people and sheep of Your pasture,
will give You thanks forever.
Psalm 79:13

How precious is Your lovingkindness, O God! Therefore the children
of men put their trust under the shadow of Your wings:
Psalm 36:7

For with You is the fountain of life;
in Your light we see light.
Psalm 36:9

C

My voice You shall hear in the morning, O LORD;
in the morning I will direct it to You, and I will look up.
Psalm 5:3

_____

_____

_____

_____

_____

_____

_____

_____

_____

_____

_____

_____

_____

_____

_____

_____

_____

_____

_____

_____

_____

_____

_____

In Your presence is fullness of joy;
at Your right hand are pleasures forevermore.
Psalm 16:11

LORD, I have loved the habitation of Your house,
and the place where Your glory dwells.
Psalm 26:8

The LORD will give strength to His people;
the LORD will bless His people with peace.
Psalm 29:11

The LORD will command His lovingkindness in the daytime and in the
night His song shall be with me—a prayer to the God of my life.
Psalm 42:8

My soul, wait silently for God alone,
for my expectation is from Him.
Psalm 62:5

Exalt the LORD our God, and worship at His holy hill;
for the LORD our God is holy.
Psalm 99:9

We are His people
and the sheep of His pasture.
Psalm 100:3

Rest in the LORD,
and wait patiently for Him.
Psalm 37:7

As the deer pants for the water brooks,
so pants my soul for You, O God.
Psalm 42:1

The LORD is my shepherd;
I shall not want.
Psalm 23:1

He makes me lie down in green pastures;
He leads me beside the still waters.
Psalm 23:2

C

Before the mountains were brought forth, or ever You had formed
the earth and the world, even from everlasting to everlasting, You are God.
Psalm 90:2

He is our God, and we are the people of His pasture,
and the sheep of His hand.
Psalm 95:7

The LORD is my rock and my fortress and my deliverer;
my God, my strength, in whom I will trust.
Psalm 18:2

He makes my feet like the feet of deer,
and sets me on my high places.
Psalm 18:33

Mercy and truth have met together;
righteousness and peace have kissed each other.
Psalm 85:10

LORD, You have been our
dwelling place in all generations.
Psalm 90:1

I will instruct you and teach you in the way you should go;
I will guide you with My eye.
Psalm 32:8

He loves righteousness and justice;
the earth is full of the goodness of the LORD.
Psalm 33:5

Trust in the LORD, and do good;
dwell in the land, and feed on His faithfulness.
Psalm 37:3

Delight yourself also in the LORD,
and He shall give you the desires of your heart.
Psalm 37:4

My soul longs, yes, even faints for the courts of the LORD;
my heart and my flesh cry out for the living God.
Psalm 84:2

For a day in Your courts
is better than a thousand.
Psalm 84:10

C

Trust in Him at all times, you people;
pour out your heart before Him; God is a refuge for us. Selah
Psalm 62:8

Whom have I in heaven but You?
And there is none upon earth that I desire besides You.
Psalm 73:25

Oh, taste and see that the LORD is good;
blessed is the man who trusts in Him!
Psalm 34:8

Your mercy, O LORD, is in the heavens,
your faithfulness reaches to the clouds.
Psalm 36:5

But He made His own people go forth like sheep, and guided them in the wilderness like a flock;
And He led them on safely, so that they did not fear; but the sea overwhelmed their enemies.
Psalm 78:52-53

So we, Your people and sheep of Your pasture,
will give You thanks forever.
Psalm 79:13

How precious is Your lovingkindness, O God! Therefore the children
of men put their trust under the shadow of Your wings.
Psalm 36:7